WITH LOVE TO MY HUSBAND, SKIP JEFFERY, WITH
WHOM I ENJOY EXPLORING THE WORLD — S.M.

ACKNOWLEDGMENTS

The author would like to thank the following people for sharing their enthusiasm and expertise: James E. Kelley Jr., coeditor of *The Diario of Christopher Columbus's First Voyage to America, 1492–1493* (Norman: University of Oklahoma Press, 1989), and a member of the Council for the Society for the History of Discoveries; Lieutenant-Colonel Douglas Peck, retired United States Air Force officer and respected ocean navigator, who conducted the first-ever field study of Columbus's first voyage by sailing solo across the Atlantic; Keith Pickering, author of research papers on Columbus's navigation and consultant to the National Geographic Society on Columbus's first voyage; and Dr. Thomas Tirado, professor of history emeritus, past professor of Latin American history, and head of Millersville University's Columbian Quincentenary Project, an internationally supported online database of journals, correspondence, and media reports regarding Columbus and the legacy of his voyages.

Book design by Jessica Dacher.
Typeset in New Renaissance and Requiem.
The illustrations in this book were
rendered in chalk pastels.
Manufactured in China.

10 9 8 7 6 5 4 3 2 1

Chronicle Books LLC
680 Second Street
San Francisco, California 94107

www.chroniclekids.com

Library of Congress Cataloging-in-Publication Data
Markle, Sandra.
Animals Christopher Columbus saw: an adventure in the new world
by Sandra Markle; illustrated by Jamel Akib
p. cm.
ISBN: 978-0-8118-4916-6
1. America—Discovery and exploration—Spanish—Juvenile
literature. 2. Animals—America—History—Juvenile literature. 3.
Columbus, Christopher—Juvenile literature. I. Title.
E112.M363 2008
970.01'5—dc22

2006033623

...ALS Christopher Columbus Saw

An Adventure in the New World

by Sandra Markle   illustrations by Jamel Akib

chronicle books · san francisco

Note to Parents and Teachers

The books in the Explorers series take young readers back in time to share explorations that had a major impact on people's view of the world. Kids will investigate why and how the explorers made their journeys and learn about animals they discovered along the way. They'll find out how some animals affected the outcome of the journey, helping explorers find their way, causing key events to happen, or helping the explorers survive. Young readers will also learn that, because of the explorers' journeys, animals were introduced to places they'd never lived before, sometimes with dramatic results.

The Explorers series helps students develop the following key concepts:

From the National Council for the Social Studies:
Human beings seek to understand their historical roots and to locate themselves in time. Such understanding involves knowing what things were like in the past and how things change and develop. Students also learn to draw on their knowledge of history to make informed choices and decisions in the present.

From the National Academy of Sciences:
Making sense of the way organisms live in their environments will develop an understanding of the diversity of life and how all living organisms depend on the environment for survival.

CONTENTS

A Race for Riches

Would you believe that, once, worms inspired people to explore the world? In fifteenth-century Europe, silk made from the thread of silkworms was more valuable than gold. Silk and silkworms could only be found in the areas now known as China and Japan, and finding the fastest sea route between these areas and Europe could make an explorer very rich. Christopher Columbus was determined to find that route. In 1492, he set off with three ships, and while he did find land, it wasn't what he expected. Neither were the animals he found along the way.

For centuries before Columbus's journey, explorers had been leaving Europe in search of new lands. When they returned from their expeditions, they brought things back from the cultures they visited, including spices like pepper and cinnamon, which made foods taste great and kept them fresh. The people of Europe became very fond of spices. They also liked silk, a shiny, soft cloth spun from threads produced by silkworm caterpillars. Unfortunately, both spices and silk came from faraway lands called Cathay (KATH-aa) and Cipangu (chi-PON-gu), now known as China and Japan. They also came from islands south of Cipangu that Europeans called the Indies.

PERSIA

ARABIA

AFRICA

INDIA

THE SILK ROAD

CATHAY

CIPANGU

Spinning Worms

Silk is made from threads produced by a kind of moth caterpillar. The caterpillar produces these threads in order to spin itself a cocoon. Inside the cocoon, the caterpillar changes into an adult moth. But to make silk, the cocoon is dropped into boiling water before the caterpillar becomes a moth. After the cocoon is boiled, the silk threads are carefully unwound. As many as 3,000 cocoons are needed to produce enough thread to weave just 1 yard (0.9 meter) of silk.

SOUTH CHINA SEA

To reach Europe, the silk and spices had to be carried by
caravans of camels across deserts in Africa, packed on horses
and mules over mountain trails, traded by many different merchants,
then finally sent by ship to Spain, Portugal, and other parts of Europe.

The Moors were people who ruled northern Africa. They charged
the caravans a fee for crossing their land, and because different Moorish
rulers controlled different regions, the Europeans had to pay many fees.

SHIPS OF THE DESERT

Camels are especially suited for hauling goods across dry, sandy deserts. Their wide footpads keep them from sinking into the sand. Their long eyelashes keep blowing sand out of their eyes. The fat reserves in their humps break down, giving off hydrogen that combines with the oxygen they breathe in. Together, these elements create water. Camels can go several weeks without drinking.

FOLLOW THOSE BIRDS

In Columbus's time, sailors believed seabirds, like gulls, roosted on shore every night. So when sailors could not see land but saw seabirds, they thought land was nearby. That belief would affect Columbus's voyage. However, the sailors were wrong. Some birds, like arctic terns, travel long distances across oceans for many weeks between their winter and summer homes.

FROM IDEA TO PLAN

The European kings and queens knew the silk and spices could be transported by sea much faster and less expensively than by land. Columbus, who was born in Italy in 1451, was determined to find a sea route from Cathay and Cipangu. He believed this was his chance to become rich and famous. And he thought he knew just the route to sail.

In the 1400s, Europeans knew only the parts of the world that they had sailed to and explored. No one knew that a whole continent—now known as North America—existed to the west between Europe and China. In addition, Columbus believed the world was a rather small place. He thought the Indies were closer to Europe than they are.

THE NIÑA, PINTA, AND SANTA MARÍA

For more than eight years, Columbus tried to sell his plan for a sea route to the rulers of Portugal, England, France, and Spain. Finally in 1492, King Ferdinand and Queen Isabella of Spain agreed to give him the money he needed. They gave Columbus three ships for his voyage: the *Niña* and *Pinta*, two fast sailing ships, and the *Santa María*, a larger, slower freighter.

CATS AND RATS

Rats were a problem on most ships. They produced many, many babies that ate up all the food stored on board. To keep the rats under control, ships rarely went to sea without cats.

On August 3, 1492, Columbus's fleet set sail, but they didn't take a direct route. Heading west from Spain would have launched them straight into winds that would blow against them. By sailing south to the Canary Islands first, Columbus's ships caught winds that pushed them west. As they sailed, the crew often trailed lines to catch fresh fish for dinner, so they were well fed.

But not everything was going well. The sailors soon discovered that the *Pinta*'s rudder—the part of the ship used to steer—wasn't working properly. After only four days at sea, it broke. While the ship still sailed, the crew hung over the side and fixed the rudder temporarily. Luckily, the ship reached the Canary Islands safely and permanent repairs were made. On September 6, 1492, the fleet set sail again. This time they headed into uncharted waters.

SARGASSUM WEED

BABY CRABS

BABY TURTLES

GO WITH THE FLOAT

Baby turtles swim long distances to
reach the Sargasso Sea. Then they
stay for years while they grow bigger.
They ride on the floating weeds, hide
from predators, and eat lots of tiny
snails, crabs, and shrimp.

CROSSING THE GREEN SEA

On September 17, Columbus saw bunches of green weeds floating on the waves. Two days later a booby landed on the ship. The sailors were excited. Maybe this meant land was nearby!

Days later, the ships sailed into what looked like a gold and green meadow of floating weeds, an area that is now called the Sargasso (sar-GAS-oh) Sea. The men spotted young crabs on the weeds and again believed this was a sign that they were sailing closer to land. But they were wrong. The Sargasso Sea is a nursery for many young sea animals. They eat the plants and one another until they grow up. Small fish come to feed on the young sea animals. Dolphins and bigger fish, like sharks, come to feast on these fish.

BABY EEL

THE SARGASSO FOOD CHAIN

In the Sargasso Sea, just about everything is eaten by something else. The turtles float among the sargassum weed and feed on tiny snails, crabs, and shrimp. The mahi mahi feed on the turtles, and the mako shark feeds on the mahi mahi.

MAHI MAHI

MAKO SHARK

Are We There Yet?

When two more days had passed with no land in sight, the men began to grumble and argue about heading home. But Martín Alonso Pinzón, captain of the *Pinta*, silenced their complaints when he reminded them that they should keep going because they were sailing for the king and queen.

On September 25, the seamen spotted what looked like an island in the distance. Some of the sailors were so happy they jumped into the sea for a swim. Dolphins leapt around them and darted among the three ships. But by the next day the celebrating was over. The men realized that what they had seen was just the shadow of clouds on the sea.

THERE SHE BLOWS!

At about this time, Columbus wrote in his journal that he saw a whale spouting. It may have been a gray whale, as they are still seen along the route the discovery fleet traveled. Growing to be 35 feet (10 meters) long, a gray whale would definitely have been easy to see from a distance. In fact, it would have been just 16 feet (5 meters) shorter than the *Niña*, Columbus's smallest ship.

It's a Sign

Finally, at 2:00 AM on October 12, 1492, Juan Rodriguez, on board the *Pinta*,
shouted, "Land ho!" They had spotted land—truly this time! Shortly after dawn,
the landing party climbed into the *Pinta*'s small boats and headed for shore.

Christopher Columbus leapt out of his boat ahead of all the others and waded onto
the beach. There he dropped to his knees and gave thanks for a safe voyage. He named
the new land San Salvador and claimed it for Spain. Neither Columbus nor the Spanish
rulers cared that a group of people Columbus came to call the Tainos (TI-nohz) had
already settled on the island and called it Guanahaní (Gwah-nah-hah-KNEE).

LIZARD LUNCH

Guanahaní was also already settled by lots of animals. One, the curly-tailed lizard, was only 7 to 10 inches (18 to 26 centimeters) long. Bones found at Taino village sites show the lizard was sometimes on the Tainos' menu. Columbus may have seen and eaten this lizard.

While the sailors did not speak the Tainos' language, they managed to communicate that they wanted to trade for the Tainos' gold jewelry. The Tainos were very interested in the sailors' mirrors, bells, glass beads, and red cloth caps because they had never seen anything like them before. When the landing party headed back to the ships, several of the Tainos chased after them in dugout canoes, carrying things they thought might be valuable enough to trade: spears tipped with fish bones, cotton, and colorful parrots.

Columbus ordered his men to capture six of the natives. In his logbook he described them as strong, healthy, smart, and likely to be good slaves.

PARROT IN A PALM TREE

The parrots the Tainos brought to trade were probably Cuban parrots. They are noisy, colorful birds. Columbus was so impressed that he took a pair home to the queen. Today the population of Cuban parrots, like many other kinds of parrot, is shrinking. That's because, just like Columbus, many people capture these birds to be pets.

27

THE WILD NEW WORLD

For the next two weeks, Columbus's ships went from island to island. Along the way, Columbus reported seeing parrots flying in flocks so large they blocked out the sun. Whenever the ships stopped in villages, Columbus's men traded for gold and searched for spices and silk. They kept looking for Cathay and Cipangu, thinking they were just beyond the Tainos' islands.

FRIGATE BIRD

BOOBY

CUBA

JAMAICA

SCARING UP A MEAL

As he island-hopped, Columbus saw frigate birds and boobies. Boobies dive into the water to catch their food. Once a booby finishes its meal, a frigate circles and attacks, frightening the booby so much it coughs up its food. The frigate then swoops down and grabs the thrown-up glob out of thin air.

PAINTED FISH

For dinner, Columbus and his men caught colorful reef fish. To Columbus, the fish looked as if they had been painted a thousand ways in bright shades of blue, yellow, and red.

ATLANTIC OCEAN

ISPANIOLA

PUERTO RICO

MERMAIDS?

At one point, Columbus wrote that he and his men saw three ugly mermaids! In fact, they were manatees. Manatees are related to elephants and have fat bodies, wrinkled faces, and whiskered snouts. Every day they eat an amount of plant material equal to about 20 heads of lettuce!

BABY TURTLES

One night, Columbus and his crew discovered big female loggerhead turtles plowing slowly across a beach. The sailors captured several to eat later. They also dug up the turtles' nests and collected the eggs. Female loggerheads lay about one hundred eggs and produce about four nests during mating season. When the baby turtles hatch, they head to the Sargasso Sea.

For months, Columbus sailed through the islands of what is now known as the Caribbean, searching for Cathay. He hoped to make it through all the islands, but strong winds made the going rough, especially for the slower *Santa María*. Because the *Pinta* was the fastest of the three ships, it went on ahead. Perhaps her captain, Martín Pinzón, hoped he would find the route to Cathay first.

The *Niña* stayed with the *Santa María*. When the ships came upon an island that was larger than most of the others, Columbus named it Española (ES-pun-yol-uh). Today it is called Hispaniola (HIS-pan-yoh-luh). When Columbus arrived, the leader of a large village gave him a valuable gift—a gold mask—and invited Columbus's crew to a big feast. The menu probably included roasted rock iguana, whose meat Columbus described as white and tasty. Rock iguana grow to be about 3 feet (0.9 meter) long.

THE *SANTA MARÍA* SINKS

The *Niña* and the *Santa María* waited at Española for the *Pinta* to return, but it did not come back. Finally, on December 24, 1492, Columbus ordered the two ships to set sail. Suddenly, around midnight, the *Santa María* jerked to a stop. It had struck a coral reef, a ridge of coral just under the surface of the water. Columbus ordered the *Santa María*'s large masts to be cut down. He hoped this would lighten the ship enough for it to float off the reef. But the tide lowered and the *Santa María* sank down onto the reef. The sharp coral punched holes in the ship's wooden hull.

Animals Sank the Ship

Coral reefs are really large groups of animals called coral polyps. Each coral polyp produces a hard skeleton around itself, forming a little cup it can hide inside. Neighboring coral polyps link their skeletons together. When they die, their skeletons become the foundation on which new coral polyps build. Slowly, the coral colony becomes big enough to form a reef.

Word of what had happened to the *Santa María* quickly reached the village leader on Española who had invited Columbus and his men to the feast. He sent men in canoes to help the sailors escape the *Santa María*. They carried the men and the ship's supplies ashore.

Columbus decided that the *Santa María*'s sinking was God's way of telling him to found a colony on Española. His crew collected wood from the *Santa María*'s hull and used it to build a fort that Columbus named La Villa de Navidad in honor of Christ's birthday.

On January 4, 1493, Columbus left most of his crew at La Villa de Navidad and joined the crew of the *Niña*. He left his crew with weapons, seeds, and as much food as could be spared. Columbus promised his men that he would return to rescue them as soon as he could.

RATS OVERBOARD!

In addition to his crew, Columbus probably left a colony of rats on Española. When the *Santa María* sank, many rats on board would have swum for shore. Others hiding in the supplies were probably carried ashore by Columbus and his crew.

THE DANGEROUS TRIP HOME

On January 6, the *Niña* finally reunited with the *Pinta*. But the *Pinta* was in trouble too. Its hull had been damaged by shipworms and was leaking. Columbus had not completed his mission, but he worried that if the fleet kept going, he might lose the *Pinta* too. He decided it was time to sail home.

It was a difficult journey. Twice the fleet sailed through storms so fierce the men thought the ships would sink. And the *Pinta* and the *Niña* became separated. After they lost sight of each other, they traveled on alone. Neither Columbus nor Martín Alonso Pinzón knew if the other ship had survived.

SHARK!

In good weather, the *Niña*'s crew trailed baited lines behind the ship and caught a huge shark. That provided enough fresh meat for several days. Because of its size, the shark was probably a great white. Some grow to be as much as 23 feet (7 meters) long. Imagine what a job it was to haul that huge shark on board!

Thinking his ship, the *Pinta*, was the sole survivor of the discovery fleet, Martín Alonso Pinzón stopped in the Spanish port of Bayona. There he sent a letter to King Ferdinand and Queen Isabella, claiming Columbus's successes as his own. He asked permission to meet them and share his discoveries. But the rulers had already heard that Columbus was alive and on his way home. The *Niña* and the *Pinta* both returned to the Spanish port of Palos on March 15, 1493. A short time later, Martín Pinzón became sick and died.

WINGED WELCOME

Columbus's men knew they were back in Europe when they went ashore and saw white storks soaring overhead. The birds' nests, nearly 6 feet (1.8 meters) wide, were also a familiar sight on rooftops, chimneys, and church bell towers.

A World Changed Forever

Sometime in the middle of April 1493, Columbus traveled to meet with King Ferdinand and Queen Isabella. He led a parade of his men, showing off some of the things they had brought back from the Caribbean: gold, their Taino captives, and strange animals.

Columbus didn't know that he hadn't made it to the Indies. He was convinced that he needed to sail only a little farther through the Caribbean Islands to reach Cathay and Cipangu. He would later go on three more voyages but would never find the sea route he hoped to discover. His explorations were still important, however. His voyages helped people understand that the world was a much bigger place than they had imagined. Columbus also helped bring about the exchange of plants, animals, and, unfortunately, diseases across the Atlantic Ocean. For better and for worse, his exploring would change the world forever.

CUBA

HISPANIOLA

SP

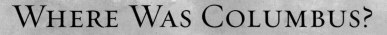

AFRICA

ARABIA

PERSIA

INDIA

CATHAY CIPANGU

WHERE WAS COLUMBUS?

Columbus never did make it to Cathay or Cipangu. Many people have tried to figure out where he did land on that first expedition. All they have to go on are the compass headings and distances traveled that Columbus listed in his logbook. Based on these, they believe Guanahaní could be one of several islands in the Bahamas: the western cay of the Plana Cays, Watling Island (now San Salvador), or Samana Cay. Or it might also be Grand Turk Island.

GLOSSARY

caravan   a group of travelers crossing a desert or other harsh environment together

current   a large mass of flowing water or wind

fleet   a group of ships sailing together

hull   the body of a ship without its masts and rigging

logbook   a record of daily events

Moors   a name that was used broadly to mean both people from North Africa and people of the Muslim faith

navigate   to sail a course from one spot to another across water

reef   an underwater ridge of rock or coral near the surface of the sea

rigging   the ropes supporting a ship's masts and sails

rudder   a flat upright piece attached to a ship's stern that can be used to make the ship turn

spice   any of a number of vegetable products, such as pepper, used to flavor food

Taino   the name given to any of the native people living in the Bahamas

voyage   a journey, especially one taken across the ocean

FOR MORE INFORMATION

To learn more about Christopher Columbus and his voyages of exploration, check out these books and videos.

BOOKS:

The Discovery of the Americas: From Prehistory through the Age of Columbus (The American Story), by Betsy Maestro. Harper Trophy, 1992.
Investigate the many different people and explorers who "discovered" the Americas, from prehistoric times through Columbus's landing.

Follow the Dream: The Story of Christopher Columbus, by Peter Sis. Knopf Books for Young Readers, 2003.
Through beautiful illustrations and text, follow Christopher Columbus's life from early boyhood to his first landing in the Americas.

If You Were There in 1492: Everyday Life in the Time of Columbus, by Barbara Brenner. Aladdin, 1998.
Explore what it was like to live in fifteenth-century Spain, when Columbus was growing up and planning his voyage to the Americas. Discover what people ate, how they dressed, what it was like to go to school, and more.

VIDEOS:

Biography: Christopher Columbus. A&E Television Networks, 2000.
See Columbus's rise to fame and his decline. This account shares rare art, artifacts, and interviews with experts on the man, his voyages, and the time in which he lived.

Great Adventurers: Christopher Columbus and the New World. Kultur Video, 1999.
This video tells the story of Columbus's life and effort to fulfill his dream against great odds.

INDEX